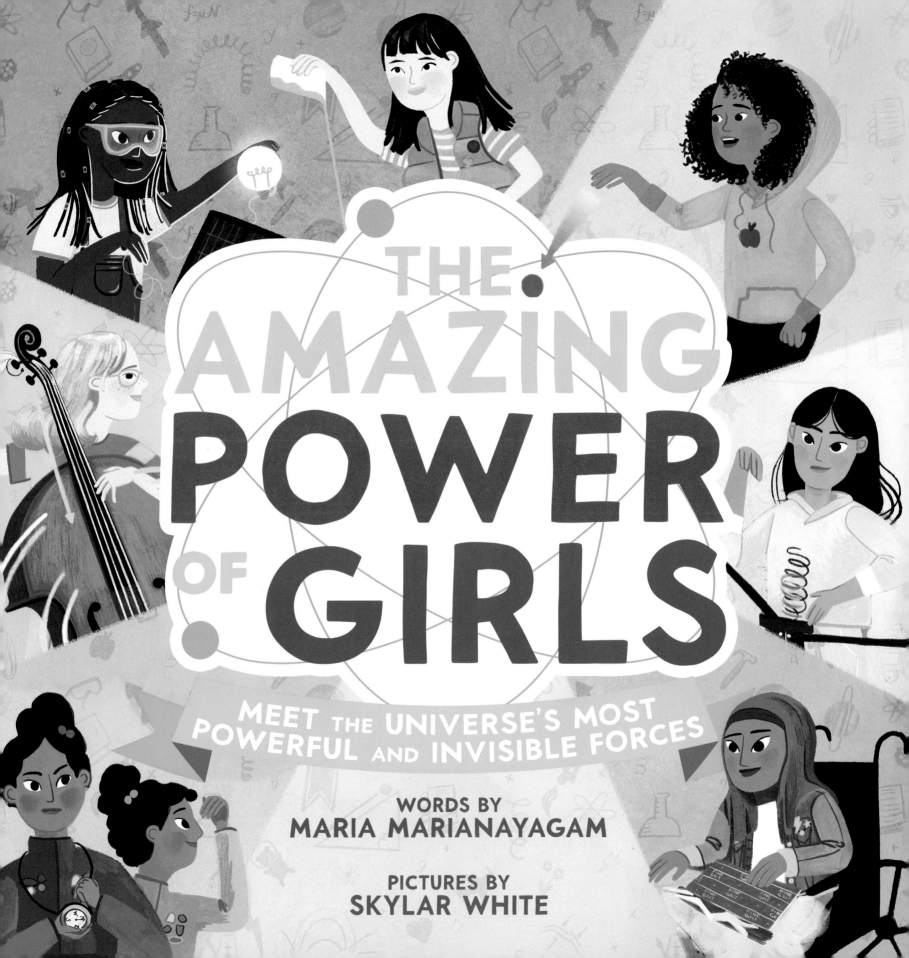

THE AMAZING POWER OF GIRLS

MEET THE UNIVERSE'S MOST POWERFUL AND INVISIBLE FORCES

WORDS BY
MARIA MARIANAYAGAM

PICTURES BY
SKYLAR WHITE

For Eliza, Anna, Gabriella, and for you, the forces that will change the world.
—MM

To my mom, who always encourages me to take risks.
—SW

Published by Sourcebooks eXplore, an imprint of Sourcebooks Kids
P.O. Box 4410, Naperville, Illinois 60567-4410
(630) 961-3900
sourcebookskids.com

Cataloging-in-Publication Data is on file with the Library of Congress.

Source of Production: Wing King Tong Paper Products Co. Ltd., Shenzhen, Guangdong Province, China
Date of Production: November 2023
Run Number: 5035943

Printed and bound in China.
WKT 10 9 8 7 6 5 4 3 2 1

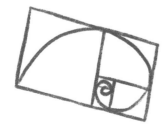

THE AMAZING POWER OF GIRLS

WORDS BY
MARIA MARIANAYAGAM

sourcebooks
eXplore

PICTURES BY
SKYLAR WHITE

I am a force
to be reckoned with.

I am gravity.

Pulling you in undeniably.

gravity

I'm grounded,
holding all in place.
Leaving it behind
when I'm in space.

I'm down-to-earth.
I'm a guarantee.
The apple doesn't fall
far from the tree.

I am buoyancy.

Find me in any lake, ocean, river, or sea.

Floating, bobbing, lifting up,
supporting you, won't let you drop.

Lighthearted, I go with the flow.
Feel weighed down? Just let it go.

buoyancy

I resist wrong, and I push back.
Won't let it slide, won't get off track.

I create the definitions.
Unmovable in my mission.

I am magnetism.

A powerful and electric rhythm.

I am charming. I compel you.
Charged with energy, I propel you.

I motor, motor, motor, around.
I guide. I grip. When lost,
I've found…it!

I am tension.

Pulled in different directions.

Keeping things straight and tight and fixed,
but falling apart with one big hit.

When under pressure, cut me some slack.
I need to rest, repose, relax.

I am nuclear.

Follow me, your group leader!
An atomic force that's hard to sever.
A strong force, holding it all together.

I generate power, strength, and light.

A star, all day and through the night.

I am a spring.

Push me down and feel my upswing.

I'm hooked on harmony; I like my rest.
I'm up and down, I must attest…
I'm sometimes stretchy, sometimes stiff.
I enjoy my downtime;
I enjoy the lift.

I apply myself and I can't be stopped.

I push, I pull, lift up, and drop.

When I grow and build momentum,

I'm the **F**orce that **MA**kes it happen.

Come at me with all your might.

And I'll come back, with equal fight.

Forces are an essential part of our everyday lives. Although we cannot physically see forces at work, they are present, and they are everywhere.

I am a force of nature, but what does it mean when I say I am...

Gravity? It means you are the force that pulls objects in. Earth's gravity pulls everything—including us—toward it. It's a force that's always present. It keeps everything in place and prevents it all from floating away. Legend has it that a scientist named Isaac Newton discovered gravity when an apple fell from a tree and hit him on the head. He realized then that there must be some invisible force pulling it toward the Earth. All matter in the universe has a gravitational pull, but the more massive the item, the stronger the pull. Have you ever seen footage of an astronaut bouncing on the Moon? That's because the Moon is smaller and lighter than the Earth and therefore has a smaller gravitational pull. In fact, Earth's gravity is six times stronger than the Moon's, which means if you weigh sixty pounds on Earth, you will weigh only ten pounds on the Moon!

Buoyancy? This means you are a force pushing up. Buoyancy is a force that exists only in fluids: liquids like water or gases like air. Buoyancy is why you feel so lightweight in the water—it's what helps you float! Have you ever tried to push a beach ball down into the pool water? The force pushing against you is buoyancy; it wants to keep the beach ball floating. Similarly, in the air, buoyancy is the force that keeps a hot air balloon floating in the sky. The heated air in the balloon is lighter than the air surrounding it, and this causes the hot air balloon to rise higher into the atmosphere. All fluids exert buoyancy on objects immersed in them, no matter where they flow.

Friction?

Friction? This means you are a force resisting motion. Friction is a force found on every surface. When you push a box across the floor, the force pushing against it is friction. Different surfaces have different friction levels. Ice is smooth and low-friction, which is why skaters can glide effortlessly on it. Pavement is rough and high-friction, which is why you can walk on it without sliding. Friction is important because it keeps things in place, like preventing cars from skidding on the road. Friction is a word that can also be used to describe the relationship between two people—it can describe those moments when we rub each other the wrong way.

Magnetism? This means you are an attractive or repulsive force. Magnetism is a property of certain rocks and metals that attracts or repels other metals. Magnets have two "poles"—one pole is the north pole, and the other is the south pole. Opposite poles attract each other, and similar poles repel each other. Metal can be transformed into a magnet by rubbing another magnet against it. You can also wrap metal with a wire and run an electric current through it to create a magnet known as an electromagnet. Magnetism has many uses. Electromagnetism is used to propel maglev trains in Asia! These magnets keep the trains floating over their guideways, allowing the train to travel at extraordinarily high speeds. There are also many everyday uses of magnets as well: holding your report card up on the fridge, finding your way with a compass, or creating sound vibrations in a speaker.

Tension? This means you are a force pulling a string, rope, chain, or beam in different directions. For example, the strings of a tennis racquet are kept tight using tension. A tennis player will adjust the amount of tension in their racquet according to their liking. A lower tension allows them to have more power, but higher tension means more control. But if the tension is too high, a string can break easily from a hit. You can also see tension in action in the strings of a guitar or in a game of tug-of-war. In tug-of-war, when one team finally lets go, the rope becomes slack, and the tension disappears! Tension or being tense can also be used to describe a person's state of mind—if we are stressed out, we are often tense and probably need some rest!

Nuclear? This means you are the force that holds the nucleus (the center) of an atom together. Atoms are the tiniest pieces of matter that make up all things. The center of an atom is called a nucleus, and it is made of protons and neutrons. The force that holds the center of an atom together is also called "strong force" or nuclear force. Did you know that if a heavy atom is hit by other neutrons, it can cause the nucleus to break in two, releasing a significant amount of energy? This is known as nuclear fission. If this energy is harnessed safely, it can be used to provide power and electricity to our homes. Nuclear fusion, on the other hand, is when two lighter nuclei merge to form a single nucleus. This reaction releases an even larger amount of energy than fission. Nuclear fusion is what powers our Sun and stars.

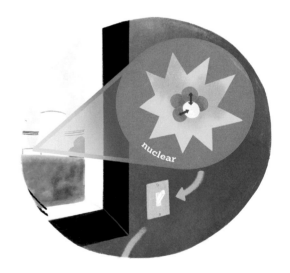

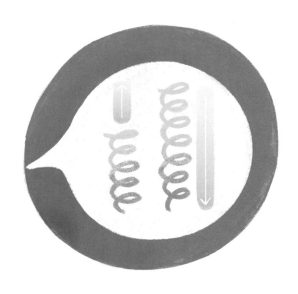

Spring? That means you are the force of a spring trying to get back to its resting position. If a spring is pushed down, it will bounce upward. If it's stretched up, it will coil downward. A spring will bounce up and down until it gets to its resting position. A spring's movement is defined by how much weight is acting on it and how elastic or stiff it is. This is called Hooke's Law. A slinky is an example of a very elastic spring, whereas the spring that launches a pinball into play is quite stiff. Bungee cords, windup toys, and even the keys on a keyboard all use spring force. If a spring could move back and forth forever—stretching to the same point and compressing to the same point every time—it would be in perfect harmony, a movement called harmonic motion.

Applied? This means you are just being you. Applied force is the force of you on an object. Pushing, pulling, picking up, and dropping are all examples of applied forces.

The last stanza of this story also expresses Newton's three laws of motion:

I'm the **F**orce that **MA**kes it happen.

1. An object will remain at rest or continue to move unless acted upon by another force.

2. Force is equal to the **mass** (total amount of matter) of an object multiplied by the **acceleration** of the object (how quickly the object speeds up). $F = m \times a$.

3. To every force, there is an equal and opposing force.

FURTHER READING

If you would like to learn more about forces, you may enjoy the following:

Diehn, Andi. *Forces: Physical Science for Kids*. Nomad Press, 2018.

Swanson, Jennifer. *Explore Forces and Motion: With 25 Great Projects*. Nomad Press, 2016.

Choney, Suzanne. "Why Do Girls Lose Interest in STEM? New Research Has Some Answers—and What We Can Do About It." Microsoft, May 2, 2018. https://news.microsoft.com/features/why-do-girls-lose-interest-in-stem-new-research-has-some-answers-and-what-we-can-do-about-it/.

Hill, Catherine, Christianne Corbett, and Andresse St. Rose. "Why So Few?" American Association of University Women, February 2010. https://www.aauw.org/app/uploads/2020/03/why-so-few-research.pdf.

Author's Note

Dear Reader,

I have loved math and science since I was a little girl. My dad is an engineer, and I was always fascinated by the work he did, and he always supported my interest in these subjects. When I grew up, I decided to follow in his footsteps and become an engineer myself. When I started my first year of engineering, however, I was shocked by how few girls were there with me. I wondered if, perhaps, other girls hadn't received the same encouragement to pursue a science career that I had. And I wanted to change that!

For the longest time, STEM (Science, Technology, Engineering, Math) education has focused on boys, especially in engineering, computer science, and technology—so much so that some of the women's restrooms in my engineering faculty were just old closets turned into bathrooms as an afterthought!

High school physics is required to pursue engineering, and the forces discussed in this book are a big part of physics. I hope from reading this book, you can see how amazing forces are! They are invisible and yet so powerful. And sometimes, as girls, we may feel invisible, yet we, too, are so powerful. So, this book is here for two reasons. One, to teach you forces in a memorable way and remind you how fun they can be! And two, for you to realize that just as every force has its own unique purpose in the world…so does every girl. You are the most important force. You can do anything. So, let's be the force that changes the world.

Dear Parent, Guardian, or Educator,

A great deal of research has been completed about the gender gap in STEM careers. The good news is that studies indicate a few things:

- that if parents or teachers communicate STEM to girls early, they are much more likely to be interested in these subjects in the future;

- and if girls feel confident about their STEM abilities and they, as well as others, believe in their potential, they are more likely to pursue a STEM career.

This is great because girls are critical to STEM careers. Girls problem-solve differently than boys do, and both ways of thinking are needed to develop good, safe designs. I hope this book will help introduce girls to physics and make them feel like the powerful forces they are.